# The Second Longest
# Day of the Year

**Also by Jean Prokott**

*The Birthday Effect*

# The Second Longest
# Day of the Year

## Jean Prokott

HOWLING
BIRD
PRESS

2021 Poetry Prize Winner

Howling Bird Press
Augsburg University
2211 Riverside Avenue
Minneapolis, MN 55454
612-330-1125

http://engage.augsburg.edu/howlingbird/

Published 2021 by Howling Bird Press
Printed in the United States of America
Book and cover design by Jim Cihlar
Cover art: *Timetable,* Erica Harris
The text of this book is set in Adobe Garamond Pro and Acumin Pro Condensed.

First Edition

21 22 23 24 25 5 4 3 2 1

ISBN: 978-1-7365777-1-4

This book is printed on acid-free paper.

*for 1224 Highland*

*and for Brian*

## The Second Longest Day of the Year

### The First Lie Your Mother Tells You

### Suddenly There's a Whistle

## This Is the System by Design

The Sundog Captured in the Shot

# The First Lie Your Mother Tells You

# The Birthday Effect

*You (yes, you) are 6.7% more likely to die on your birthday.*

when I die on my birthday,
which is the day after the first day
of summer

it will be the second longest day of the year,
which is good
because you'll have more time
to mourn.

in June, the sun is the same color
as the birthday candle's flame
that jerks from its waxy perch,

and the day melts to dusk,
which gathers in plastic pools
on the landscape of buttercream.

when I die on my birthday,
there's .00018% chance it'll
be because I fell out of bed that morning

or 1.6% chance it'll be suicide,
because God, I hate my birthday
ever since my mother threw me a party

and we played that game where
you sit on balloons until they pop
and you win if you pop the most—

I remember wearing all pink,
standing stubborn in the grass
while girls I sort of knew

from school popped and giggled
and popped and little latex
empty rainbow gall bladders
scattered the front lawn.

oh, I thought that was so stupid
and my mother tried so hard.
we hit the piñata with a yardstick

and everyone *had fun*
but I just gathered my candy
like beach shells that all were beautiful
and retreated into myself
and wanted to never
birthday again.

when I die on my birthday,
it probably won't be suicide.
I think I'll get shot by a toddler—

those gremlins kill 52 people a year—
or I'll fall off a boat and hit my head
on the side (626)
and my blood will mix

with the pastel circles of gas fumes
because people are often
on boats in June, at dusk, swatting

mosquitos, which also might be
what kill me (1 million),
or when I die on my birthday,
it will be when I accept the cancer

because hey, I've reached a milestone
so might as well quit while I'm ahead
before it erodes my bones (1,550)
or my breasts (40,610)
or my colon (50,260)
or my lungs (157,423)
or my eyes (330).

and when I die on my birthday,
celebrate the day after the year's peak,
the highest sun,

the first day of descent.
put all my birthdays in a museum
or plant them as trees

or fill the gall bladders
and send them to the sky

## I Am a Salmon, I Am Not a Salmon

A company called *Whooshh*[1] created a vacuumed tube, and they called it the Salmon Cannon,[2] and without it we would surely have a salmon famine.[3] The fish swim toward the circle-tube-end, which obviously represents a vagina,[4] and reverse-birth themselves home, which is the place they've been looking for the entire time.[5] Before the Salmon Cannon, there were Salmon Stairs,[6] a Salmon Truck,[7] and a Salmon 'Copter,[8] but nothing was so fast as the Salmon Cannon,[9] and nothing so misty,[10] and nothing so fun. If we do not cannon, stair, truck, or helicopter the salmon, they swim into turbine blades[11] and are chopped into fishy bits, and if they are not chopped into fishy bits, they stare up, see 551 feet of dam,[12] and think w*ell, hell, where are we supposed to go now?*,[13] because they've imprinted on the other side, where they were born.[14] So, the lady salmon lay their eggs in warm water, or they lay no eggs at all, and they swim in circles.[15] But at the Roza Dam,[16] salmon find the 150-foot tube in groups[17] and are sucked in together,[18] stretch 100 feet high, and pop out the other side[19] in this new birth.[20] The fish fly, slippery like pineapple spears, and they are home, and maybe someday they will be snatched by bear or pinched in eagle talons and flown high above the earth, just one more time.[21]

---

[1] It sounds like it sounds.

[2] They must be poets.

[3] I am a poet.

[4] I am a literature student, too.

[5] I am a salmon, too.

[6] And at the salmon gym, a salmon stair-climber.

[7] Not driven by salmon.

[8] Not flown by salmon.

[9] 22 mph.

[10] Like your thumb over the garden hose when you make rainbow, rainbow, rainbow.

[11] If only someone would cannon me away from the blades—but I am not a salmon.

[12] Salmon can see ultraviolet light, which humans cannot; salmon can see beyond the violet.*

    *Beyond the Violet* is the perfect salmon band name.

[13] How many times have I said this, too?

[14] I drove by my childhood home, and the lawn needed to be watered.

[15] Their slick bodies are moving crescent moons.

[16] In Washington.

[17] I would only travel the Salmon Cannon with you, fin in fin.

[18] The tube can carry 40 fish at a time.

[19] Like a tennis ball out of a ball machine.

[20] When they hit the water, it is a second baptism.

[21] Because with every birth there is every death.

## The Birthday Effect

at the gender reveal party,
the plane crashed and
      the pink water
made red mud and nothing else.

at the gender reveal party,
      the forest burned
—not blue—not pink—
but like poorly mixed Tang,
brown like a fresh heart unfolded,
      artificial maple air.

(what is the gender of trees
if not fire)

at the gender reveal party,
the cannon to shoot
pink or blue powder
exploded and killed
the father-to-be.

    *

      when is the appropriate time

      to tell the child
      *child, we set it on fire*
      *because of you*

child, you have no choice
but to unwrap this
catastrophe.

# Big, Fat Pregnancy Lies

The Union soldier was shot through his testicle
and the bullet lodged into the fallopian tube
of the woman standing behind him. Virgin
birth, he does the right thing, marries her.

The 1920s rabbit test: inject your urine under the white fur.
If she lives, no baby, if she dies, you'll convince yourself
you can feel the baby moving inside of you.
You're afraid to sleep stomach-down.

The Atlantic states in 1934: girl swallows octopus egg.
She cramps in her gut, feels the pinch like someone
has tied her intestines in a knot and keeps pulling tighter.
Eight tentacles grow. Somewhere else, a girl pregnant from the pool,
who knows who the father is. His sperm swam through the chlorine—
hounds looking for a scent.

1965, the great New York blackout, the *zhoom* of the great
unplug, the refrigerator stops humming, then
heavy-breathing-groping in the dark, hot breath on a tender neck,
limbs intertwined. *Let's do it again, the lights are still out.*
All those babies nine months later, born of darkness and boredom.

And when it's a mistake, the *shake and shoot* method. Coca-Cola
spermicide, Dr. Pepper douche. Put your thumb on the bottle
and shake, spread your legs, stuff the lip of the bottle inside.
When you're done, you can get 5¢ return.

Or, maybe you should've tried girl-on-top, or sex on the rag,
or maybe you should've taken 20 aspirin afterwards,
or jumped up and down, your bare, flat feet hitting hard,
or maybe you should've sneezed after.

The first lie your mother tells you while you've got a mouthful
of watermelon, a snowball of pink dripping down your chin:
*if you swallow a seed, you'll grow a watermelon in your belly.*
Your stretch marks zebra like the thick, green rind.

## Sonnet for the Summer

My students open their eyes, find light, breathe
with unripe lungs, develop sex organs
they then think with, become round bodies with
layers of donut glaze; they grow toenails,
grow more on my hot nerves. I'm far enough
along in this year I can't remember
the woman I was nine months ago: young,
showered, suntanned like red ale, gazing at
berry-clustered stars. Rochester, baby
bump of Minnesota, umbilical
cord, nutrients from me to students. Soon,
it will be June again. I will swaddle
them in linens, send them back to their real
mothers, and break, alone, from the cycle.

# I Return an Email

[Re: poop]

Last month, you literally peed your yoga pants from laughing too hard, and I told everyone. Next year, you will graduate. Then you'll move out, then you'll say something cruel to your best friend, then your cat will die, then you'll interview for a job in an awkward suit, and then, some random day, say, your wedding day, you'll pull your gown's silk and lace over your waist and think back to the day teenage-you decided to email your teacher *poop*.

Thank you for thinking of me. It is the fur you grow into, the fading spots, 11th grade, it is the decision to lick the icicle because fuck the world, it is black or white, win or lose, it is searing pain when your chin hits the asphalt, and *why would you* wear a helmet when you rode your skateboard down the 11th Street hill?

Fuck that hill. The chin scar is the *shiiiiiiiiiiiit*. Everything heals, and quickly.

The truth is when I read that email I was drunk on Jameson and wrapped in blankets. You think I am old, and you are right. Teachers have nothing to do but teach lessons and live in metaphor, so here's a reminder that history exists to show you who you are. Quit volleyball and go to the library. Vote, read *Slaughterhouse-Five* already, throw a pot, pick fights with boring strangers.

I wish someone had taught me this.

Instead, my teachers told me to look at my potential. What a lazy thing. Life is a peripheral mess. I'm telling you that one day you will wrestle creatures, pee your pants again, blame your mother for your depression, break shit, and fail to slam on the brakes, and you will collect and categorize the moments from your past you've decided to douse in flames, and you will sniff the debris like cocaine, or shake it into your cuts, or rub it into your gums, desperate for its offering. This is not meant to be a spiritual experience: it is only your homework.

Last night, I dreamt someone baked my own teeth into cookies and fed them to me. This part is a symbol. It represents what we do when we become who we are.

# The Obituary

Redwood Falls Gazette: *Kathleen Dehmlow (Schunk) was born on March 19th, 1938 to Joseph and Gertrude Schunk of Wabasso. She married Dennis Dehmlow at St. Anne's in Wabasso in 1957 and had two children Gina and Jay. In 1962 she became pregnant by her husband's brother Lyle Dehmlow and moved to California. She abandoned her children, Gina and Jay who were then raised by her parents in Clements, Mr. and Mrs. Joseph Schunk. She passed away on May 31st, 2018 in Springfield, Minnesota and will now face judgment. She will not be missed by Gina and Jay, and they understand that this world is a better place without her.*

ginaandjay understand/ we grow from little stems/ that mothers nurture or drown/ ask yourself/ how will you live your life/ when your mother dies/ (how do you live your life/ because she is dead?)/ The only thing ginaandjay say/ is It's Different/ which is code for I Don't Care/ which means What Will You Do About It/ But Kathleen has something to say/ about the dim light present in us/ and her shadow/ which had gone for a joyride/ which she sewed back on/ to try to be/ herself again/ She was broken too too broken/ no more a hurricane than cirrus clouds would be/ She wasn't flying just running/ away/ The sunset was rotting/ into the horizon/ the spiderwebbed storms were warning her/ She was training her happiness/ by whispering/ what it wanted to hear/ And when she saw/ the last days of her life/ when she heard the monologue/ from life's groom/ she needed to know/ if she was a good mother/ If going by the definition/ provided/ then/ no/

# The Women Are Taking So Long in the Bathroom

misting perfume/ patting makeup/ squeezing blackheads between red-painted, dull-bitten fingernails/ washing brushing curling straightening volumizing dyeing/ poking breasts' hard spots/ shaving Brazilian-bikini-zone-red-rash-bumps/ putting tampons in/ taking tampons out/ smoke-clouds of red in clear water/ bleeding for the last time/ brown-string clumps in clear water/ looking down before flushing/ urinary tract infections/ never shitting/ peeing on white sticks/ losing clusters of dark blood/ practicing *no worries, I'm fine*/

## Weird Anatomy

one time I saw my literal fat    (it's called the hypodermis)
it was marbled    (a jaundice-colored brain)
just a little blood    (cherry glaze)
the cut a three-inch hangnail    (the fat hiding underneath the flap)
you probably want me to say    ("my God, was it beautiful" but)
it was disgusting    (acini de pepe suspended in Jell-O)
six stitches hid it    (an L-shaped scar remains)
underneath the blood stuff    (there is so much padding)
what if it were wires    (silver popping circuits)
it'd be better to have electricity    (to keep me warm)
so I'm sorry for this body    (I'm not the one who made it)

## What We Need to Speak

*"They're out there protesting what they actually wish would happen to them sometimes."*
*—Medal of Freedom recipient Rush Limbaugh, on women protesting sexual harassment*

We cannot speak without lungs.
Rush Limbaugh's were toast. His hate set them on fire—
       hate like the small, soft cherry
at the end of a man's cigar leaving ash      in his wake.

We can speak without ears. Rush was nearly deaf.
You can speak without a nose. The stuffy sound
will reverb in your head like you're both on the phone and live on air.
      When a Black woman made him mad, Rush told her
      *take that bone out of your nose and call me back.*

We cannot speak without courage      when it's to a room full of men
about birth control access.      Rush said we wanted taxpayers to pay for us
to have *so much sex*      we couldn't *afford all that contraception.*
      We say *you're not listening. That isn't how it works.*

I'll speak about my body for a second. There's a fibroid
in the smooth muscle of my uterine wall, too small for my doctor to feel. I'm fine.
Most women have them, at some point.

      Is it too cruel to call a dead man a pus-sy polyp?
His stage four tumor was three inches long, and speaking of three inches.
We can speak without a dick. Rush smuggled Viagra in another man's name.

We can speak without signs, but I'm out here, protesting again.

You can't speak when you're dead.
So Trump gave him the Medal of Freedom.
Medal means      remember what he said.

We cannot speak without a tongue, and a woman bit off a man's tongue last week.
She'd told him      you can kiss me      but don't use tongue.
      They found it in his bedroom and fined her a thousand bucks.

Maybe in the afterlife, Rush will finally bite his tongue.

You can't speak when you're dead, unless they let you.
We're telling you                    *remember what he said.*
We're telling you.                        *Remember what we said.*

## Senryū: How to Vote

oval                    small black bean
penned      clitoris                tired eye
mark        inside the lines

# Seventh Grade Science Project

Seventh grade, science project, my partner Theresa tells me *we're doing abortion*
and shows up in my dining room with glue, glitter, a cardboard trifold,

mock-fetuses that fit in her hand, and baby Holocaust photos: piles of dead
babies, sacks of boneless flesh like laundry gathered with a bulldozer,

dented, veiny blue heads like rotting cantaloupes, hollow, black circles
where eyes should be—a baby costume I could pull over my face

so my own eyes peeked through. She flips through the propaganda
like it's *Teen Beat,* she points and says *this is the vacuum they use to suck*

*the baby out of you.* I'm twelve, I've never heard of abortion, she hands me
a red marker and says *I'll glue pictures on, you color blood.*

# The Abstinence-Only Sex Ed Teacher Attempts the New Curriculum

your penis is a weapon
you must clean it quietly
like a tip-toe
you must clean delicately
so it does not go off unexpectedly
you may only fire when God tells you
it is time to go to the shooting range

> *how do I know when it is time to shoot*
> *what is the target          what is a bullseye*

it is God's weapon He will tell you

> *is everyone at war fighting with a penis*
> *is war a total sausage fest*

war is God's way of calibrating Man
your vagina is the storefront of a kitschy specialty shop
it is open at the most inconvenient times
nobody can come in no matter how long
he stands outside and taps his foot and looks
at his watch

> *then why does this shop exist*
> *what is the sales tax on the items inside*
>          *do employees get a discount*

window shopping only

so your penis is a balcony
an unsteady terrace
your vagina is a pliers          no your vagina
is a cup     it is the Lord's cup
your vagina is a five-star hotel
it has a beautiful lobby with lighting like crystal origami
you can only afford it on your honeymoon

*when my boyfriend kisses me I feel confetti in my brain*
*I feel glitter in my underwear*
*my vagina is an umbrella closing after the rainstorm*
*love is that moment when you wink up at the sky just to be sure*
*the rain has really stopped*

there is no glitter in heaven
heavy petting is saved for the animals
if you have sex your penis will be covered
in pus like days-old bacon grease        and sores        oozing
after sex your penis is a banana     the skin peels back
a triangle-toothed demon lives inside

your penis will burn      you will burn      don't have sex
don't think about sex        don't touch your penis

it is a hot stove it is acid it is a sharp knife it belongs
to the Lord      He will dust for fingerprints
when He gets it back

if you have sex       your vagina will become inflamed
it will become an open wound    infected

you will get pregnant you will
have a sin-baby  God will punish you
God will punish your child

> *why do we have penises and vaginas*
> *why did God make glitter*
> *how much does hell hurt*
> *but what if we do have sex        what if we just have to*

your penis is a sunburn
your penis is unwieldy
your vagina is a prophet
your penis is an indistinguishable signature
your vagina is a messy room

your vagina is an immigrant
your vagina is a saucepan
your penis is a shoehorn
your penis is a bridge
your penis is a car accident

  *what is* your *penis*
  *what is* God's *penis*

God's penis is your penis
God's penis is my penis

# Ghazal for the Pill's 60th Birthday

*this incubator is overused / because you've kept it filled / the feelin' good comes easy now /
since I've got the pill*

As a girl, Smarties are my pretend medicine. I swallow slick pills
like my mother: place it on my tongue, sugar, dissolve, pink, pill.

As teenagers, the cool girls carry Covergirl powder compacts in their jeans.
I follow, buy a shade too orange, carry its plastic disc in sync, my pills.

As long as the blood moon rises, we click the shell's center dial like the spinner
from *The Game of Life*. Find the day, the number, the placebo trick pill.

This is not a womb. This is not a brood bitch in a heat cycle. This is a woman.
She's free to work, learn, and fuck around. She can choose hormones (synthetic): pills.

Get rosaries off ovaries and laws off bodies. RBG's dissent. We still protest this shit.
They can't force us to be barefoot & pregnant at the kitchen sink: cheers, clink, pill.

## Love Letter to IUD

I don't think about you
unless I am thinking
about you.
You fit into the palm
of my doctor's hand:
a bird, wings stretched,
on-the-go dental floss,
hairpin,
small missing piece
from a child's toy.
She shows me
on the 3D model
how you will form
a perfect $T$ in my uterus,
a girl finding
her balance on a beam.

# Suddenly
# There's a Whistle

## Suicide Train

**1.**

I recognized a ghost in a recent obituary, a man I went on two dates with ten years ago. It's the thin blond hair that triggered the memory. He'd kissed too hard. He'd tried to convince me to climb into his backseat in a bowling alley parking lot and then begged. He was drunk, and I said goodnight—left him there with his car, knowing he would not call a cab or a friend.

**2.**

There are mysteries in our lives we don't know need to be solved, but then I saw him with that obit summarizing his 38 years. Since our last date, he'd stayed with a corporate job, gotten married, had a couple of sons, and had taken, at some point, a nice picture: smiling, round cheeks holding glasses, boyish face. Then, he took his life, and that is all I know.

**3.**

   I promise I am not trying to hijack his story.
   I am just wondering when he'd boarded the Suicide Train.

**4.**

You see, the Suicide Train is driven by the Grim Reaper in a conductor's uniform, silent and striped. We're all at the station some point in our lives, but only some of us have tickets. I've always had a pink ticket in my pocket, and when the train screeched its brakes in front of me, I had no choice in the matter—the Suicide Train *choo-choo chooses you.*

Once I boarded, the *chugga chugga chugga chugga* was the diesel of my heartbeat. I have been riding for some time, but you don't have to get off the Suicide Train, ever. Sometimes you sit in the caboose and order a sidecar, or you wander the aisles, or you half-read a novel and drift off to sleep, or you sit in the dining car and pull on your hangnails while you wait for that little iceberg salad with four croutons to come, or you take a short nap in the coffin-sized sleeper cabin. Most of the time, the trip is so smooth, I don't realize I'm riding.

I like the little salad and fall asleep while reading every time.

5.

Yet, sometimes, I watch the green world pass out the window and wonder
how to be part of it from this side of the glass, clutch my gut and bend over in
hot, numb pain, and heave sobs until my throat is scraped raw like a fish just
filleted.

This comes from nowhere: suddenly there's a whistle.

Like most of us, I'm still on the train. It is an idea, that's all. The train tracks
move through the clouds, down into the sea, across prairies and up mountain
forests. I keep the possibility of getting off the Suicide Train locked in my
chest, in morbid comfort. *Just in case, just in case.*

Some of us do that, have travelers' insurance.

6.

But some of us—some of us jump off. When it happens, Suicide Train riders
emerge from our small cabins, watch our companions open the door, feel the
wind pull, and put one foot outside and then the other. We reach for them,
mouths agape, while the wind whips at our hair, but we only see the blur of
their fall.

7.

Those days we set fire to the Suicide Train even though we know it will never
burn. We are fine with the smoke. We say, *goddammit, we are burning this
down for you. I tried to burn it down. We understand, but you've gotta come back.*
I don't even know you, but I know sometimes the door handle catches your
eye.

8.

I dreamt of him last night, baby-fine hair. We carry matches. I carry
matches . . .

# Fatty, Fatty, 2 x 4

*for my middle school bully, who died by suicide*

can't fit through
the bathroom door

    actually, we're on the bus
and you can barely fit

    bully, bully,
    we were haunted
    by the same monster,
    and he wanted us to die.
    you had powers, used them for evil.
        who found you, hanged?
        you tied your magic cape
        around your neck.
    I put my head down
    and smelled my garlic sweat.

fatty, you can't fit in the seat

look at your rolls
you can't zip your coat

    I need a pesticide for my shame—
    or just any poison.
    what do I remember about you,
    Noah?—I was on the bus first,
    you found me in the back.
    I watched your sneer, your red gums,
    as you walked down the green aisle.

here comes the bride
all fat and wide

fatty, fatty, pants too tight
look at all that cellulite

I think she has her period
I can smell it

fatty, fatty kill yourself

you could eat
all of McDonald's
lunch ladies fear her
fatty fatty want some candy
drink this Slim Fast first

look at her
she doesn't walk
she waddles
fatty, fatty kill yourself
she's going
to get blood on the seat

        I stopped eating for a while,
        I learned to run, and I did it at night
        so no one would see.
        my God, stereotypes are lazy.
        my God, I'm tired.
        bully, Noah, did your future dead self
        find you one day, to give you a reason?
        mine did. I tried a knife,
        made thin, red stretch marks
        on my wrist that scabbed over
        like Morse code embroidering,
        I tried pills, drank charcoal.

        Noah, Noah, two by two
        the animals are boarding you
        your ark, your ship, afraid to drown
        your water, your spaceship, your sky
        your ghost, your monster

            fucking stop it
            what did you do
sticks and stones
your buried bones
my buried bones
            I'm telling my mom
            but I've got a beautiful face
oh look you made her mad
            I understand
            and I am so, so sorry.
your noose, your ship
what you didn't know
about the undertow

what we didn't know
about the undertow

## How to Vanish

we begin as circles

        then become ovals and cylinders and polytopes and
                bipyramids and trapezohedrons and

        if we're lucky
           great dodecahemidodecahedrons

the doctor hands me a pie
             chart
               divided
                    into carbohydrates and
                       proteins and fats

      says *just get in shape*    and I diagnose myself    with shape-itis
                           a tragic rhombus

what I wouldn't give
                     to be skinny isosceles
or equilateral              [Bermuda]

        magnetic fields        spin my compass

    my corners are not acute              but obtuse

# How I Met Beethoven in the Psych Ward

1801, and Beethoven writes a note
*to* the pianist: *senza sordino* through
this first movement, these pianissimo triplets—

treat your whole notes like casual puffs
on a cigarette, hold on until you're ready to let them go.
No *accelerando,* only more notes,

narcissistic triplets, obsessing over themselves, one-two-three,
tripping over phrases, developing, then giving
up, like procrastination.
                    In *quasi una fantasia*

Robbie played me *Moonlight Sonata* on the yellowed
keys of the Yamaha upright in the dining hall,

settled the creak of the bench, watched his foot find
the pedal. He pushed his hospital ID to the middle of his forearm
until it stretched, and began to chop a melody, *forte.* Forcing

the notes, common time. The left hand more anxious
than the right. I blinked hard at these awkward rhythms,
these up-and-down-stair climbing notes. Not at all what Beethoven

intended. Not what Rellstab heard as he walked along
Swiss Cantons in the moonlight, not what he saw as a boat
floated like music on Lake Lucerne. When Robbie missed

an accidental, he pounded his palm flat on the keys.
*Keep going* I told him, and closed my eyes to this unrehearsed
interpretation. Because everything is beautiful

when they don't let you leave. Even among the grunts
of a frustrated stranger, I drowned in Beethoven's
love-song-argued-funeral-hymn.

I was 17. This was about me. This is about me.
He pinky-plucked the song, the triplets repeating,
the weakest three fingers of his right hand forming the melody—

the weakest part of him creating this music—
which as written looks easy, yet is so hard to play.

# I Hate to Break It to You, but a Dollhouse Is Just a Coffin

and a coffin is just a universe.
inside, there is a smaller you
who bends only at the waist and never
the knees. you rearrange celestial
furniture—a couch, a refrigerator
with a tiny jug of milk inside, a bed
like a pink brick. Kierkegaard said
every choice we make ends a life we
didn't live. yesterday's dead yous
married someone else, committed
insurance fraud, learned to play
drums. tomorrow's yous might get
drunk under a streetlamp, have a kid,
find a plot hole. there are as many
dead yous as there are stars, trillions
& trillions of farewells—so crack open
this clamshell and your doll can live
each life, dizzy with freedom. force her
narrative, smooth her hair, change her
plastic shoes, once you fish them out
of the vacuum. unhinge your house
like Mary's palms and take a leap of
faith. look through the peephole of
this kinetoscope and find your infinite
timelines. one plays violin, two waltz,
another boxes. others hide in rooms
with no doors. and you wonder, but
about *You*. the choices I made. well,
those will fade into nothingness in less
than a century. but now, right now,
there is this life that made the cut. this
is the life we will celebrate. when the
dirge plays, when the mourners find
their way, they will see the landscaping
Smaller Jean has planted, my funeral
flowers, which explode into fireworks,
inkblots, crooked lines, and color.

## Don't Calculate the Number of Funerals You'll Eventually Attend

Don't calculate the number of funerals you'll eventually attend. Especially if your family is Catholic on both sides. Spoiler alert: you will spend your life haunted by circumstance. Spoiler alert: here's the story in reverse. Dénouement: your father survives the quadruple bypass. Climax: the final black stitch is put into place. In the rising action the doctor tells you ad nauseam *your father is a ticking time bomb*. But we are all ticking time bombs and our rising action is the wires: if you cut an orange you have to cut a red, and if you cut a black, you cannot cut a green. In the exposition, your father is shoveling snow, and you aren't paying much attention. Look, I know you want to kill time by thinking of your parents dying, but I don't suggest this. This is why I've stopped answering the phone and stopped waiting for answers.

## Sonnet for Another Birthday

Ming, the mollusk, was 507,
and he died when Icelandic researchers
pried him open to see how old he was:
we cannot age clams unless they are dead,
we cannot count our rings once they've blended;
we all live in our gray, calcareous,
chalky shells, hold mysteries inside us
that are emancipated when we die.
So let's promise we'll be better this year.
Start by imagining Ming back on his
ocean floor, his hard wings closed, cradled in
sediment—before we scooped his story,
pulled him through the weight of water, spread him
open, and probed his speechless, meaty tongue.

## The Anointing of My Father

He takes Confession first, so we leave the room.
I joke that we'll put our ears to the door and listen to his sins.

When we return, we pray over my father. The hospital priest
wears a small, purple neck sash, which is part of the travel-anointing-kit

he carries on his person. The other tools: oil in a small vial
on his keychain, communion wafers in a compact

mirror. He washes his hands, and the walking mini-mass
commences. Everyone is scared, except for the priest, who asks us

to bow our heads. We make small signs of the cross over our hearts.
I whisper the Our Fathers.

# Study for Jean d'Aire

*In 1347, during the Hundred Years' War, King Edward III approached the starving citizens of Calais: to save themselves from a massacre, six members of the council must volunteer their lives as well as surrender the key to the city. With bare feet, six volunteers walked to the English camp and presented themselves. At the negotiation of Edward's queen, the men were spared. In 1884, French sculptor Auguste Rodin was commissioned to sculpt the event* (The Burghers of Calais), *and Rodin chose to portray the men in the moment before they left the city. Jean d'Aire was the second of the volunteers.*

someone sick, someone lost, someone finds
the mute study of Jean d'Aire in the subway
of Mayo Clinic, alone, in between two plants,
at the bottom of the stairs, his body hunched
forward, his oversized arms bearing his weight,
his geological, patient frown.

     and aren't there bones under this bronze

when they trail their fingers across his caved, cool chest,
wrap their hands around his soft fists, as is the divine
tradition when one hears news or has a moment of light,

when they too, know nothing of what is to come,
when they hear Rodin: *the body, weakened by suffering,
still holds on to life, is consumed by bravery.*

     and isn't this an act of bravery itself,

to look for an explanation in the pensive eyes
of a man, heavy with decision, married to mud and time,
to ask, if they themselves might be cast bronze,
if they might clench air and wait for the final rendition,
the one where they embrace the large key to the city,
that beautiful patina key—

isn't it an act of courage to wait with Jean d'Aire
for a new self to be smoothed into place
by the geometric, calloused tips of an artist's thumbs.

# The Loneliest Birthday in the Galaxy

*The first song played on another planet was "Happy Birthday," hummed by the Mars rover Curiosity to celebrate the anniversary of its landing. However, because there was no scientific gain from a singing robot, it was Curiosity's only celebration.*

Curiosity hums in EDM,
a little *arpeggio* at the end,
208 million miles from home.

and my God I wish
I could go to its party,
put on a triangle hat,
zoom to the blue sunset,
invent new words for dawn.

a day on Mars
is a sol.
a year on Mars is 688 sols, or 1.88 Earth years.
so 88% more presents.

what does one get a robot
for its birthsol? perhaps
two rising moons—
Phobos, the giant walnut,
Deimos, the warped skull.

if a robot hums "Happy Birthday"
into space, does it make a sound?

Curiosity celebrates like a drunk undergrad—sends robot selfies back to Earth
        @MarsCuriosity #nofilter #powerhour #arerobotsalive #birthdayeffect

my God I'd love to be there,
hiding my footsteps in its tire tracks—this is when it carried me—
on the butterscotch of Mars.

how many different ways can you begin something?

Curiosity sings his Nintendo tune,
but he doesn't have a candle for his cake.

since there's only 0.1 % oxygen on Mars,
he can't sustain a flame.

## NASA Shows the Deepest Ever View of the Universe

Are we supposed to see these failed art projects
God shoved in the back of his closet, painted after
he crashed the Caravan, Pollocked for his Girl,
later found on the brown and white tile
outside her locker the night of the school dance?
His work on Earth is well published, anthologized. This art:
innards of a Funfetti cupcake after a bite,
rock candy luminescence, grade school years' finger paints,
a watercolor on the back of a Dear John letter. He wishes
he still painted. Years from now, after the divorce,
his children will find the Universes creased and coffee-stained
in an old Chuck Taylor shoebox. They tenderly unfold them,
careful of the flaking egg tempura paint, worried they'll crack
the only parts of him they don't know.

## Ritual

When surgeons opened my father's chest,
they found me, sleeping, and offered
a scalpel porch.
Metal clamps split the world down the middle.
I climbed to the slick surface of his heart and watched
his flat, quiet lungs set in his ribcage sky.
        There are poems everywhere about
the presence of blood in blood, about the levers
we pull in each other's chambers, which we navigate
        from memory. Together,
we prayed for the soft, breathing pinks of dawn.
I did not leave, and he did not ask me to.

# Philoso-tree

I've been trying on Pantheism
for the last couple of weeks, pulling
on the philosophy one leg at a time

like everybody else.

I'm trying to find God in everything,
and it's always the last place you look.

God didn't make the world, he is the world.
Point at something. That's God!
Spinoza said he was "God-intoxicated."

Man, I'd love to be drunk
on holy.

But obviously, God is mostly trees,
because every time I tell my students
to turn a concept into a metaphor,

they turn it into a tree. Grammar is a tree.
A poem is a tree. Hamlet is a tree!
Every goddamned thing's a tree—
branches like neurons reaching for pain
or pleasure, leaves, from green to yellow.
Students go deciduous every time.

Pantheists believe in universal substance:
both intelligence and matter, and it creates

out of itself. I can't see it.
I can only imagine more "me"s

coming off me, blonde heads bubbling
and splitting skulls in mitosis.
I can only imagine God

hiding in his tree, peeking out through a small
eye slit in the trunk. He has been assigned

the nonspeaking role of "tree" in the school play.
He is sweating under his costume,
waiting backstage for his cue call.

## The Ghost of Christmas Past, Who Looks like Your Father

Your father is still living,
he is alive, he is alive.
Every day, when he gets home from work,
he opens the snaps of his shirt
and there is coarse hair on the globe of his gut
and a new scar on his chest. If you connect
its dots, the scar is a red,
wounded Christmas tree.
But the Ghost of Christmas Past
Who Looks like Your Father
wears a flame of white light
where the hair should be and moves
like steam. Its spine is fish bones
under the fluttering curtains of its robes.
Someone says, *you have your father's shadow.*
If you die first, you'll haunt your father
with light. No one you love is dead.
Your house is made of bones
from the living, which they sacrifice:
a limb and a limp for a place to grow.

# Oh Dear God, Another Poem about Trees

Yesterday on public radio: an interview
with the guy who updates the leaf foliage maps.

He drives up I-35,
circles a lake—
which is looking less glassy
and more giant cataract—
and bends down

like the goddamned King of Nature

to judge fallen leaves.
Brittle like an old wine cork means
less Big-Bird yellow and more
last week's macaroni & cheese,
and a rubbery bend means maroon.

He pulls out his fall map,
a Paint-by-Number,
and he algorithms how long
until those hidden reds
flare up like endometriosis.

and I'm like

*fuck you, Leaf Guy.*
*that's the best job ever.*

How is there a job in this world
to watch every tree explode
in puberties of paint
and tell listeners like me—*hey,*
*moron, go outside*
*and look at how beautiful this is*
*at exactly [this time] in exactly [this place]?*

And this morning on public radio:
it is now legal to compost human remains.

We can lay our bodies
on wood chips, alfalfa, straw—

and in a month become two wheelbarrows
of soil.

A tree can grow from my bones.

We can follow maps
to find each other.

Today, he looks at trees,
and he tells us when they're dying.

Tomorrow, I'll look at graves,
and I'll tell you when they're living.

## Another Grief Poem, Dear Reader

There are many things I want to write poems about
and none of them are grief. But here we are again,

dear reader, lying in bed, watching the star projector
circle its fuzzy shapes across the ceiling. It is a toy meant

for a toddler. My husband bought it after our dog Lenny died,
and still two years later, when I know the bad news,

I wipe its dust, plug it in, and follow the crescent moon,
shaped like a banana, as it disappears and circles back.

*Here comes the banana,* I say. Sometimes, to be funny, my father
says, *I have a good memory, but it's short.* I wonder if I too suffer

from this affliction. All you can hope for is a highlight reel
as you lay dying. Until then, hold your grief in your hand

like a quivering, hot star. Grief, hand, banana, star.
The projector turns, turns, muffled heartbeat

waves. Banana, fear, star, grief. May I be alone?
Reader, could you be a dear, could you give me a minute?

# This Is the System by Design

# Birthday Deer, 2020
Mylar & Carrion

It's a beautiful summer day. The dead
deer has been on the hill for a week.

Today, we see someone has tethered a silver and rainbow mylar balloon
around its hoof that commands *Get Well Soon!*

My husband says it's a prank, and I say it's an art installation called
*Keep Calm and Carrion.*

We've just celebrated my birthday with a masked dinner on a patio—
our first time out in four months. The southern states have opened

and closed again. A family has Covid after a pot-luck birthday.
Floridians protest face masks at a community meeting:

*You're obeying the devil's laws. In the beginning, God formed man out of the earth
and breathed his breath into him. You're throwing God's beautiful breathing*

*system out the door.* Elijah McClain was suffocated, murdered, by police
last year while we weren't paying attention. Now we learn his last words:

*I don't even kill flies. You are beautiful and I love you.* The universe speaks
to us in metaphor because we too easily deny the literal,

because we're lazy and earmuffed. The deer's neck is folded,
the head is backwards, and it hums like the Lord of the Flies. I imagine it

in a gallery, flies bouncing behind the glass, its stomach filled with helium.
The patrons smile in passing and the glass stifles the voice of the Beast:

*Why things are what they are.* There is much to think about.
Why things are what they are. Getting well soon.

## America, America, America

There was that 4th of July when I was especially overweight
and blasted Ray Charles' "America the Beautiful,"
the one with the *snare, snare, snare* at the beginning

from my apartment kitchen window, and my neighbor, the one
who smoked long cigarettes and let the staleness of them
fog, fog, fog like poison through my vents yelled

*YEAH YEAH YEAH TURN THAT UP* to me from our driveway.
She pumped her fists. I was embarrassed she could hear it,
but it was a sort of intimacy. It was eight in the morning.

I was about to mosey to the train station to eat pancakes
flipped at me by men wearing colonial uniforms in the 90 degree heat.
The sun grilled a burn, burn, burn into my neck, flags from houses

rested like white, wet shirts on a line. At the station,
I bought a Coke in a glass bottle. In the park, children ran
shoeless, pointed at boats in the bay, cheered *BOAT BOAT BOAT.*

# Pandemic Planner

schedule sadness by the minute: how many minutes can you budget per day,
is there room for joy, and if you can squeeze in joy, you have to squeeze in
guilt, because they're going to talk. organize hours like the old photographs
you should have scrapbooked years ago, organize your weeks like your closet,
rehanging them like the work clothes you haven't worn for months and
that are now pilling, tired flags. maybe you can use this time to get your tax
documents in order, to get your cans of vegetables in order, to get your affairs
in order, just in case you have an unscheduled meeting with a virus that has
penciled itself in. so, when was the last time you looked at your life insurance
policy? when was the last time you looked at your life, your marriage, your
career, the creeping Charlie spreading like a boring nuisance on the corner of
your lawn that never gets the sun?

# Quarantine with Dachshund & Labrador

the poor dog
is bleeding,

she has infected
anal glands.

we bring her
to the vet
without touching
anything

except her,
for a scratch
behind the ears.

they mend the wound
she has given herself
from biting and licking

and give her
a plastic cone.

snow on Easter

and I imagine it could
fill around her face,

make her a treat,
add fruit, sweet syrup.

in Italy, during
lockdown, drones
chase dog-walkers:

*dove vai con questi
cani incontinenti?*

where are you going
with these incontinent dogs?

the little dog
pees in my office
because he is sick
of my being home.

Brian's boss calls him:

*contract workers are terminated*
at Mayo Clinic.

hold music is also *terminated.*
an unnecessary cost.

no news
is good news
as we watch
television:
aerial shots,
mass graves
on Hart Island,
wooden and crooked
teeth, fill,

tooth by tooth,
a gaping ditch mouth,
create jaws of earth.

we take the dogs for a walk
and see a girl ride her bike
for the first time.

her mother holds
out her arms
in a phantom force field

in case the girl falls.
I steal this moment,
tuck it in my pocket.

it is the first chapter
in the handbook
for vulnerability.

back home, the poor dog,
Labrador sousaphone,
my darling phonograph.

she smashes her cone
in the doorways,
a little drunk.

I nap with her
and she twitches
while dreaming.

her sounds
are like crying.

or perhaps
they are whimpers
of chasing.

## Poem for a Healthy Body

it is advised you avoid the quarantine-fifteen/ because is stress-eating good
for you?/ fat chance/ tape the Hunger Scale to the fridge/ never reach the
10/ *that Christmas day sort of feeling*/ no/ eat quite everything/ your body
needs you/ your cinnamon roll belly button/ licorice umbilical cord/ fold
your pizza in half and it's two greasy hands/ praying/ surrender to the paper
flags/ of Hershey Kisses/ slap the sex out of your sourdough/ tame it for
consumption/ I am finished with the term *self-care*/ although I will allow
*reframe*/ as in reframe *my jeans don't fit anymore* to/ *I love my tender, red-
chafed thighs*/ reframe *am I developing a drinking problem* to/ *God Bless any
bloated chance to cheers*/ reframe your spare tire to/ *thank God I am heavy here
and not in the lungs*/ *thank God I have this soft piece of self to hold onto*/ listen
to me/ fucking eat it all/

## Head to Toe

you know the man
in the middle

of America

M
I
M
A
L

MinnesotaIowaMissouriArkansasLouisiana
HatHeadShirtPantsBoots.

some see an elf
big hat
jingle toes

and some see a chef
pot belly and hot pan
frying up some Kentucky

but canyousee his Tennessee
dick

M
I
M
    Tennessee dick
A
L

Southern boner
erect Volunteer

walk along
his Mississippi-River
stitching

but careful
not to let
your Louisianas
get wet

      Oh, MIMAL!
      MIMAL!
Great experiment,
Frankenstein's American Monster,
filthy form,
what are you thinking
of your accursed creators?

We keep
fucking it up,
      don't we

our hubris
our thoughts rambled
in the fields of paradise

you might have spoken
but we did not hear

there was no hand
stretched out

only Tennessee dick stretched out
seemingly to detain me

## Capitalism Q & A

if you need to know how much billionaires have made since the pandemic, the answer is $3,900,000,000,000. if you're not sure what $3.9 trillion can buy, the answer is 464,285 yachts, 8,660 copies of Leonardo da Vinci's *Salvator Mundi,* or your soul, which is a small uninhabited island in your aorta. the yachts have full-size tennis courts, the painting is of Jesus holding a crystal orb, the island is where they filmed the last season of *Survivor.* if you ask what does one do with all that money, the answer is bury it in your yard or up your asshole. if you're wondering what to do with $1,200, the answer is not much. if you're confused as to why your husband earned more on unemployment, the answer is why were they paying him in beans. if you're not sure what kind of people wait in line for cans of beans, the answer is people you know. if it is unclear why the economy opened so soon, the answer is this was a health emergency until we learned it was about the Black and Brown and poor. if you're wondering why billionaires are taking your money, the answer is they upgraded to the newest iPhone and they eat too much avocado toast. the answer is if they hadn't bought Starbucks every morning, they could've saved something. if you ask how come the billionaires don't save Flint, or homeless veterans, or prescription drug prices, or Black lives, the answer is how do you think they became billionaires in the first place. if you're wondering why we're protesting in the street, the answer is those people didn't have to die. if you're wondering whether capitalism is patriotic, the answer is those people were going to die anyway.

## Covid Karen

privilege is a weapon
Covid Karen carries
and her protest sign says
*sacrifice the weak.*

her roots are showing,
her country is free,
and face masks
deprive her of oxygen:
we must hear her clearly

when she calls the police
on the Black man watching
black-and-white warblers
& American crows and on

the Black man stenciling
BLACK LIVES MATTER
in chalk on his property.

Covid Karens come
from six feet on the 6th day,
made from man's BBQ rib,
happy hour special.

they rise from the ocean,
salty and seawater stench.

their bodies are peeling
decals on the back
of a minivan, white
silhouette cartoons.

we made a mistake.
in the dark, we summoned
her. found a mirror—
and isn't a mirror

a self-portrait?—flicked
a lighter, chanted
*Covid Karen* thirteen times.
and she emerged,
screaming and scratching
and ready to haunt.

## Meditations on Man & Manatee

swimming low near Homosassa Bay, there is a manatee
with *TRUMP* etched in thick font on her back. last week,

the manatee was president of herself. now, think of a man
on his knees, holding the creature down, and working

his stiff hand, whittling the president's name into the algae
on her body like a painter's tool strips wood for a new stain.

one cannot fathom. the only appropriate response is
*we must carve violence into him.*

this will not be forgiven. what does this say about humanity.
you mean *humanatee* said the poet. because what else

is there to do when we have no words besides push
language together, to dwarf it, warp it, destroy it, engrave it

into a perfect creature. letters make the words make the poet
make the monster make the man make the American. Columbus

called the manatee a not-so-beautiful mermaid. the manatee
was not discovered, so she cannot respond. *manatees are not*

*billboards,* says the scientist. but *TRUMP* is a dark, branded
race track of text, failed construction. the algae will grow back

eventually, will fill in the brutality with an emerald map.
the manatee holds America on her topographic back,

north, south, invisible Mason-Dixon. when you look
for her body, find a footprint: an oval ripple. find where

the sunlight reflects a halo into the shallow water. she
moves slowly enough so as to be baptized indefinitely.

# American Triptych

*with Chris Haven and Dean Rader*

1.
perhaps you swam to Michigan

jumped off the ferry in sweet, freezing anticipation.
or maybe you snuck through the bottom,

the open border where the lakes aren't hugging
the land with their wet wings.

perhaps you rode a horse to Michigan

across the Mackinac Bridge at night in late
February, the branches of the White Pines white

as the sky is cold, your heart never galloped so fast
so hard, you never felt the darkness pull your reins.

perhaps you are a ghost in Michigan

floating from peninsula to peninsula
following the worst weather, logging every complaint,

collecting them for the day that the snow, and everything
beneath it, will be unpacked.

2.
The air in Minnesota is the color of histories forgotten,
then erased, like boats and bogs, like dusty green,
like summer cement splashed with water. Minnesota tastes like
Kirby Puckett, like 38 hanged Dakotas, like two Indian ponies
off the highway to Rochester. It tastes like F. Scott burning
Benjamins in the Mall of America. Minnesota air sounds like
Prince's guitar, like opening Grain Belt, like cutting wheat,
like the moment when Garrison Keillor stops talking, like
what happens when everything needs to be cleared away.
What do you think the wind is for? What do you think all

those lakes are for? Or the sky above or all those birds
who pick away what's left, because we all arrive at our time
to go. Because there is another Minnesota being kept
on ice, deep below the soil layers of the mollisols,
alfisols, and histosols, where something warmer waits,
the source of rivers, because the next Minnesota will surely
come from seeds we forgot we planted. Minnesota will sprout
10,000 second chances. It will water itself from the spout
of the Arrowhead, sky-tinted, cloudy water, and we will
Scotch-tape it back together, plant a Lake Itasca thumbprint
into its landscape, and from it, the River will flow again,
winding like a stray piece of twine from the Largest Ball.


3.
California has decided to start living
more intentionally, put out all these fires,
maybe start Pilates, see someone

about the shaking in this one hand
that invented so many new shades
of forest that even the border forgot,

and California has put in paperwork to change
its state song, because "I Love You,
California" is too much of an ego stroke.

You can love yourself, but at what expense.
California put the Sierras on the market,
and I might offer over asking. A little sweat

equity, a new paint job, some solar panels,
and it will be ready to go on the market
as its own country. All it wants is for you

to want it. What would you give to live in an
idea? What would you pay to feel about a new
land the way you used to feel about this one?

## Empathy Is a Preexisting Condition

we can neither insure nor assure you,
this is the system by design. a doctor died

by suicide. we say *keep your composure.* we say
*it's not that bad.* your empathy is a cold egg,

hold it in your hands, place it in warm water,
crack it open, get rid of it, and start over. send

yourself to rehab for kindness and hope insurance
covers it. the cure is close the door and turn off

the light so no one knows you're home. post your
empathy online #nofilter. learn to respond:

*Am I My Brother's Keeper?* this is not sustainable.
one day, there will be a word for this, a national

diagnosis. some say it's *overreactive.* others say it's
*normal.* we say it's *empathy,* and only some of us had it.

# The Goodbye iPads

the goodbye iPads are fixed on four-foot-tall tripods as though they are sheet music
    waiting for a musician.

the goodbye iPads are stored in a carpeted room next to stacked chairs and bins of
    medical supplies.

every now and then a nurse has to come in, flip on the light, and see one-hundred-
    thirty faceless heads.
she selects the closest one, wraps a kind fist around its neck.

she carries the goodbye iPad to the patient's room, gently sets it in front of him.
the tripod's rubber tips make a soft thump on the linoleum, the screen lights up
    and she reaches for his hand.

the goodbye iPad is not a face, but this year it has been a hundred faces.
three faces appear to say goodbye, and then they power down. the screen becomes a
    dark mirror.

the patient's wife is at home, on her iPad, swiping through pictures, and stops at
    her favorite.
she pushes the tip of her thumb and index finger to the screen, spreads them apart
    to zoom in on his face.

the nurse has not shown her own face in weeks, except for her eyes through the
    shield's glare.
she cleans the goodbye iPad and returns it to the storage room.

newly aware, it rejoins the room of robots and finds a place in a lopsided row.
the goodbye iPads look to it, heads cocked, telepathizing *but what does it mean
    to be aware.*

## How to Be Light

be seen, or don't. be the quarter circle sun
in every child's art, rays attached
like a lion's mane to your cell of a body.

convince a man to look at you directly.

live inside our bodies, or let us put you there:
there's a very nice rumor we can inject you
through our skin. pour yourself into a syringe,

and we will tourniquet our arms.

pass through the hospital window,
create a rainbow on our brow.

lay your spectrum on beach sand
and hold our hot suffering in your ultraviolet.

# The Sundog
# Captured in the Shot

# On the 20th Anniversary of My Attempted Suicide

I add a semicolon tattoo to my floral sleeve; it's a dot and wink punctuation puncture of the almost-suicide; it says *your sentence almost ended and here's a beginning*; the semicolon could be an accident: a pair of dark moles, a vampire scar, an uncapped pen; I'd stockpiled pills; it was three days before my 18th birthday; the Prozac capsules were yellow-turquoise-shiny-plastic handfuls of Barbie doll shoes like traffic in my throat; 13 years later, we gave it a name: bipolar II; it is the mild salsa version; it is independent clauses on each side, depressed and hypomanic; I'm jumping off buildings; I'm jumping over buildings; sometimes I bird-perch on the semicolon to stay warm; I don't remember much about it, to be honest; but imagine being dead for 20 years; or alive for 20 more;

## The Birthday Blues

I came as a six-legged horse,
cobalt cold,
Picassoesque Man o' War

       carrying a jockey made
       of bubblegum and branches,
       my entire life muted fanfare,
       a race lost to Upset.

       in the race
       between woman and man
       my breasts hold me back—
       azure and cinderblock.

I came as indigo as time,
riding a balloon
the balloon was filled with glass—

I came as stiff as seized gears
I greased the pinions with acetone
the acetone was on fire—

I was born sapphire,
and I don't know why
I'm here.

I iron my cornflower cape
and question joy.

Unhappy birthday to me,
I come as an ocean,
navy and bored.
I will major in lazy

and become a galaxy—
hold stars
between my fingers

*I got baby reds*
*I got baby greens*
*I got baby blues*

## She's Just a Very Old Fish Who Has Accumulated a Lot of Things over Her Lifetime

*In Northern Minnesota, a man who was sick with a mysterious illness caught a rare fish, which was identified as a fluorescent orange bigmouth buffalo. The man said the fish brought him luck, but had he known the fish was rare, he would have let her go. She was over 100 years old,*

she was the same size as his leg,
she was the very same orange as the golden hour.
the scientist hypothesized
she's mutated
or she's just a very old fish who has accumulated a lot of things over
her lifetime.

she was the Myth, the Golden Fish, more than marlin.
she swallowed an electric grapefruit, she took a job in construction, her
favorite foods were cheese puffs and chanterelles, she was a jack-o-lantern who
ran away before the ritual carving, she, of course, harvested bright ideas, she
was half-koi, she shot-putted a cantaloupe poorly, she hoarded fireflies in fresh
butter, she said Orange You Glad I Didn't Say Banana and was cursed for life,
she morphed habanero.

don't underestimate her.
these are all true—
—she digested the sunset and captured its rays in the genie
lamp of her body—
—he killed her, he killed her, he hung her
on his wall

# Anthropomorphism

Our dogs killed a rabbit this morning.
Its scream was like a bird caw,
and I saw them tugging the toy, distinct white tail,
until they disappeared behind the garage to finish the maul.

My husband took care of it.
He held a black, heavy-bottomed garbage bag, and I imagined
the crumpled carnage inside.

>"What was it like, did they eat it?"
>"No, but they ripped its belly open. Its guts were spilling out. There's
>blood on the back fence, if you want to go see."
>We looked to the dogs, bonded pair on the couch.
>"Well fuck, that's disgusting."
>"I'm just trying to give you some imagery to work with here."

What have I done
to raise such carnivores?

Brian cracks,
"Maybe they did it for your Mother's Day gift,"

and now I wonder if this should factor in
to our decision about whether we'll have a child,
because we can't decide.

If this were a Stephen King novel,
I'd get pregnant, but it would be rabbit babies,
and they'd claw out of my uterus.
Or I'd be making my morning coffee a week later
and a bloody cotton tail and bones would fall into the pot.

Later, I scroll through my phone, and Brian asks what I'm looking at.
>"I want to know if the internet says our dogs are evil."
>He says, "I already Googled that. We're fine."

I don't let the dogs near me
for the rest of the day. I give them side eye,
whisper, "Murderer, I hate you," when they saunter into the room.
I say, "What the fuck is wrong with you" as they squint at me
from their sun-square.

I lift their lips to examine their teeth,
and they comply. And at night, they win again.

We cuddle in bed. I stroke Pepper's black fur.
We have a one-to-one, human nose to Labrador nose.
"We're not going to do that anymore, okay?"

The dachshund, Beaker, burrows under the covers,
and I pull them up to survey him in his blanket cave.
"That's not who we are," I tell him.

## Love Poem for a California Condor

The Wiyot Tribe credits him for recreating man,
the Chumash believe he flies too close to fire,
the Yokut claim he eats the moon.

He died in the wild in 1987, lead poisoning, power lines.
His head looks like a testicle, a worn, leather coin purse,
his neck changes color with mood, and when it's red, he finally
loves me back. I lower my head, accept, and we mate for sixty years.

Every other year,
I lay a blue egg.
We take turns sitting.

## Lake Superior Proposes Marriage

I'm heartbroken to tell her I'm already taken by Brian, who studies rocks for a living, who walks her shores and picks her stones, who points, names, and pockets smooth charms: *chert, gneiss, basalt, rhyolite,* the victory of *agate.* It is our second anniversary. He is handsome and unshaven, and I am dreaming. Here I am in my flannel skin. There he is, squinting at a rock that looks like a tiny planet. There she is, taking small sips of his hiking boots, leaving champagne suds in her wake.

## While My Husband Is in Foot Surgery During a Pandemic, I Watch Footage of the Lake Fire

as it chars 10,000 acres, 0% contained.
fire tornados, which I just learn exist, suck
everything inside to feed a hungry burn.
lately, we have become very good

at burning and throwing things away,
inhaling smoke damage of want versus
need. we hauled three truckloads of trash
(the rug the dogs obliterated with shit,
the bottom-rusted fire pit,
closet doors detached from the rail)
to the dump and paid the city

to take our rotten leftovers.
we found a nice rake in the dumpster
so brought it home. when we burned
leftover firewood, we accidentally
set the lawn on fire and created
a bald spot of dirt, so we used the rake
to comb the fresh grass over it. in fact,

it's my husband's toe arthritis.
his tiny bones have been rubbing
and leaking fluid: his aging's attempt
to escape his body. the cartilage
will never return. his choice is either
surgery during a pandemic, or a lost
toe and flip-flops that look wrong.
I know it's just his toe,

but the purpose of toes
is so we can find our balance
and bear our own weight.
the nation is missing its toes
and my husband will be fine.
the word *fine* is a gift.

my father-in-law sent his will
yesterday, alongside t-shirts,
a Disney ticket stub, a dice game
about pandas, and pictures of
Christmas 1996 in front of
a stockinged fireplace. *we had that
same wrapping paper,* I tell my husband.
and *wow, your father still wears those
same shoes,* which are alligator texture
and tassel. he's in Florida,
immunocompromised, has fired
his nurse, ventures to Walmart
when food runs low. in the cereal aisle,

he asks a young woman to help him
with his shoe and falls over while she
adjusts it. I imagine him in the middle
of a disrupted galaxy, except celestial
is fire, and stars are ash, and ash
is the virus begging for our lungs.

even those of us pacing at home
have lost a year, a tax write-off
of our lives. a million of the dead
have lost five years, ten, fifty.
you shouldn't talk about dreams,
but last night in mine a stranger's baby
hugged me tight. I dreamt everything
was okay and am terrified by it,
because the word *okay* is a miracle.
in his anesthesia dreams,

my husband finds Plato's World
of Forms and learns shadow isn't
enough. his body and my body
and your body will join him.
in this World, everyone is alive.

we're all walking through the forest,
we're pointing to the smoke,
and pine needles are crunching
like matchsticks under our feet.

## Plumology

hunger is the thing with feathers
and hope is the thing I don't notice
until it is too late: the dead bird
the dog holds in her mouth
like a grenade on our daily walk.

this is the same walk over the creek
we've taken the last three years:
cross the bridge, sidestep the green
tubes of geese shit—
each produces a pound per day—
and cross the parallel sister bridge
to head home.

on cold mornings, the shadows
from the bridges' architecture
are still frosted stars, a slippery
mosaic. I leveled up this winter
and bought a down coat,
a poufy, knee-length Michelin Man,
which makes it harder to bend

over as I try to pry open
her jaws, which only encourages
her to ingest bones and beak
more quickly and in furious, staccato
bites. when she's done, she hacks
a feather out of her throat. it's some
real Sylvester-Tweety nonsense.

it's the wrong kind of pride,
like when you were in kindergarten
and brought your mother
a large, gray feather, said *beautiful,*
as though you'd truly found
something. maybe you'd put it
in your hair, make a pen

or a necklace, tickle the bottom
of a foot, you had so many
great ideas.

she slapped it out of your hand,
said *disease.* it's true you can't have it,
the Migratory Bird Treaty Act says so—
a feather can cost you $15,000.
imagine the Feather Police
busting down your door
to search for any attempt
at flight.

I think it's a song swallow
she's devoured. dead enough
to be frozen solid. in spring,
they sing a song every eight seconds—
2,300 songs a day—and as we trudge
back home, the tips of grass
sticking out of shallow snow
like my neglected leg hair,
my human down,

I'm thinking the dog will now
start each day with a little
singing, a tune she has stolen
and memorized by throat,
by tail, by beak, by crown,
by nape, by breast,
by belly, by wing.

## Change Is Inedible

*a typo*

I am between
the ages of 38 and 8,000.
my wings are wood planks
and I spit up time
like Gerber peas.

indigestion of minutes
makes me a bloated
hourglass, disjointed
digital numbers.

who will we be
in 10 years, in 29, in 30.
how gray will I be,
how bald will you,
how fat will we?
how many bedsides
will we weep at,
how often will we visit
graves or hold ashes
or plant trees
            —which one of us
will die first
which one
of us will die first
which one
will miss the other
will it be
too painful to live

which one
will eat
alone—

dear, I must compost

this existential dread
to feed our vegetables.
I will thaw my memories
and heat them
like leftovers
in a buffet of time—

the recurring dream
when I have too much
dessert and never
enough plate.

we bide time
until meals consumed.
we plant our small garden
and cross our fingers
for growth.

the June strawberries
survived the rabbits,
so we pick their red teeth.
we pinch jalapeño stems
and balance wrinkled Earths
of overripe tomatoes in our palms.
we always over-plant.
some of this food
will go to waste.

together,
we harvest
          and wonder
*now what*

          *I don't know*
          *I don't know*
*but I promise*
*I'll be grateful*

# The Second Largest Ear of Corn in the World

We can see it
from our kitchen window,
and I know you're thinking
*you lucky bitch!*
At night, it's lit
from the bottom
—a rocket ready to leave this world behind—
and some nights
I crawl out the window
and board. I climb
its spindly legs,
pass the green husk,
and hike the yellow skull teeth,
which are painted
with *L*s in the corner
to mimic the kernels'
gleam. Maybe I'll dive
inside, swim in the 50,000 gallons
of water meant for all
of Rochester.
Maize God!
The unanswered
Google question asks:
*what is starting wage?*
The city wants to tear
it down, and I wish
we'd eat it instead
and see raw gums
rather than empty space.
I bought a shirt with its picture
on the front. It says *Eat Local.*
The Second Largest Ear of Corn in the World
has 4.3 stars on Google.
The one star review:
*it's not real corn.*
The five star:
*I expected nothing, and it gave me everything.*

# I Convince My Best Friends to Visit Kepler 186-f

They're calling it our cousin—
habitable orbit, same size as Earth.

You can see the resemblance:
blue smile, white eyebrows,

skin like a teenager. It takes
9,040,500 years to get there,
so you pay for gas.

Fine, we'll split it.

Once we see the road sign
that reads *Constellation Cygnus,*

we'll think we're close,
but we're not. That's like

passing into West Texas
when you're driving to East Texas.

But times, like, six.

High noon is our almost-sunset.
So you know, things are a bit different

at Kepler's. They put ketchup
on their eggs, don't make a face.

Their days last months. Their sun
shines only 10% of what our sun

shines. But it will be luminescent
for trillions of years, and our sun

has five billion years left, tops.

## Ode to Stopping

the Subaru is on its tiptoes, and my husband pries
the brake pads off the rotor.

he brings them to me—shows how I've worn them
to the metal, how I've ignored their guttural anger

of stopping. it's cold this pandemic, and I'm very interested
in staying inside. we've been warned to bring in
the newly planted herbs, and I see the cilantro agrees,
closes into itself like a long-dead spider.

the worn pad forms the pattern of Saturn's rings. I might
live in those rings, travel the superhighway around a cell
to protect it, gain speed with each lap, create a shield
from my endurance. I hate to break it to you, but human

beings everywhere believe many things that are obviously
untrue: the brakes will work every time, we're not vulnerable
to a virus, it's not necessary to check oneself for wear.

I'm embarrassed I ignored the signs
for so long. I never learned slowing down starts
with friction and requires a tremendous amount of heat.

## Prose Aubade Ending with Lipstick

a winter morning, velvet cobalt, we wait for our turn. we all consider leaving this place until May, until we're digging pockets for seeds. it might be opposite day. I think of a student's poem: *if a home is made/ a bird will use it/ if a home is not made/ a bird will not use it.* the geese never left: they honk like taxicabs when we walk alongside the creek. the crows never left: they are too busy memorizing our faces and the poets need them. I meet a friend for coffee. her hair is waves of tilled soil. she is my dear friend, the sun has risen above the unshaven hills, we are drinking coffee, we never left, we are glad for it. we flip back through last year's chapter, unfold each dog-eared memory. my lipstick stains the coffee cup lid, creates an asynchronous mouth. it says, this year, let's not crease the corners. let's instead kiss the pages to remember where we should begin.

## Love Letter to a Friend over the Holidays

Merry Christmas,
You are far away.

      Today I read

a story about a fawn
named Pippin
who was adopted

by a Great Dane
named Kate.

      Pippin is me.

Her baby spots
look like a white-out
sneeze.

      You are Kate.

The white diamond on her chest
is exactly where her heart is.

      Don't you love

how dogs are designed
this way? Don't you think

      it's odd
how humans haven't
grown a new skin

to adapt
to our environment?
No tortoise shell, no chameleon
color. Only the emotional

layer. Let's call it
the *cry-a-dermis*.

Today I read

that when a cardinal
sees himself in the mirror
he tries to squawk
his reflection away.
The cardinal does not
migrate, packs no suitcase.
He has no need to load gifts
into the backseat
of the car and worry
about tearing
the foil paper.

I learned

that when a bird
flies into your house
death is coming.
This is why nobody
invites the cardinal
home for the holidays.

Merry Christmas,
you are not here.

There are only

so many things I can put
in the care package:

poems scented
like rose perfume
and toner, recipes for soup,

a clove cigarette

       half-smoked because
it's too fucking cold here
to finish it outside,

a clipping from the local paper
about a fight between
neighbors over shoveling snow
and a privacy fence
in the front yard.

I have so many things
to tell you.

Write me back.

I will tell you what
it will be like
       when I tell them to you.

## Our Problems Are the Same Size as Us, and That's Okay

Our houses are never clean, but we're not too worried about it.
Our oil needs to be changed, and we'll do it tomorrow, or maybe Friday after work.
We're fatter than we want, but Cheetos exist, so there's nothing we can do.
Our bank accounts are embarrassing, and I'm out of fucks to give.
It only snowed two inches, so we can leave it until it melts.
We sleep in too late, but the sun has betrayed us many times.
Our student loans are blood-sucking, so we'll keep getting transfusions.
        We're hemorrhaging money anyway, casual hundos here and there.
Our animals are extensions of us, and you know what, we're not sorry for that.
        Sure, they run away. But if the gate is open, you take the opportunity.
        If the snow bank is high enough, you climb it and jump over.
        We drive around and look for each other. Bones will lure us back.

# Love Letter to the Daughter I Might Have Some Day

You are small and carry half of me
with you, but if I could have it my way,
it would be all of me. I am a selfish mother

like this. If you ask me how many times
I have questioned why I'm here, the answer will be
*ten thousand.* If I am a mother, I must tell the truth:

one time I fell in love and I wasn't.
I've said bad things about good people.
I no longer think that when we die we shut down
like our lights are unplugged forever,
because when our first dog Lenny died, I held
his body, bawled into his soft ears, and still refuse
to live without him. I am a selfish mother

like this. If you ask me where you come from,
I will answer: *who knows?* I can only tell you, daughter,
that you and me—we're animals. We eat, we sleep,
we thrash, we run and pant in our dreams. The world
is hot garbage most of the time, and I don't know
how to save you. So we hold each other tight.
We catch each other's eye and it burns

until we look away. Here is what I have given you:
the right to complain. Rhetoric. Blonde hair,
that when combed enough becomes fine like a violin bow.
Permission. An appetite for sugar in excess. A healthy
obsession with shelter dogs. Unbridled, important rage.

Daughter, you are the song before the lyrics match
the tune. You are the sundog captured in the shot.
Every day I ask you where you came from
and you answer: *who knows?*

# Notes

"The Birthday Effect" death rate statistic of 6.7% is from University of Chicago economics researcher Pablo Peña as reported in *The Washington Post* on December 29, 2014. Additional statistics are from the CDC.

Phrases from "The Obituary" come with gratitude to sophomores.

Inspiration for "The Abstinence-Only Sex Ed Teacher Attempts the New Curriculum" is from Pastor Mark Driscoll quoted in *New York Daily News,* September 10, 2014: "The first thing to know about your penis is, despite the way it may seem, it is not your penis. Ultimately, God created you and it is his penis."

The epigraph for "Ghazal for the Pill's 60th Birthday" is from Loretta Lynn's 1975 song "The Pill."

Information about Søren Kierkegaard comes from the web comic *Existential Comics,* which is hilarious and accurate, I promise. Please read it.

Information for "The Loneliest Birthday in the Galaxy" comes from the article "Why the Curiosity Rover Stopped Singing Happy Birthday to Itself" from *The Atlantic,* August 10, 2017.

Information for "Oh Dear God, Another Poem about Trees" comes from the article "From Soil to Ashes" from WBUR Boston, May 16, 2019.

"Birthday Deer, 2020: Mylar & Carrion" borrows the phrase "why we are what we are" from William Golding's *Lord of the Flies.*

"Head to Toe" borrows from Mary Shelley's *Frankenstein.*

"American Triptych" is co-authored with Chris Haven and Dean Rader, with whom I collaborated to write a poem "Manifest Destiny" style regarding our respective states. Each poet contributed to each of the three sections with the goal of portraying an outside perspective as well as a personal one.

"How to Be Light" is inspired by a speech from Donald J. Trump on April 23, 2020: "So, supposing we hit the body with a tremendous— whether it's ultraviolet or just very powerful light—and I think you said that that hasn't been checked, but you're going to test it. And then I said, supposing you brought the light inside the body."

Information for "She's Just a Very Old Fish Who Has Accumulated a Lot of Things over Her Lifetime" is from the article "Minnesota Man Catches a Mystery Fish; Rare for Its Color, Remarkable for Its Age" from ABC Eyewitness News, June 11, 2019.

"Ode to Stopping" borrows the phrase "human beings everywhere believe many things that are obviously untrue" from Kurt Vonnegut's *Slaughterhouse-Five*.

## Acknowledgments

Thank you to the following publications, in which poems in this collection originally appeared, sometimes in slightly different forms or under different titles:

| | |
|---|---|
| *Angel City Review* | "Another Grief Poem, Dear Reader" |
| *Adirondack Review* | "American Triptych" |
| *Anomaly* | "Seventh Grade Science Project" |
| | "Senryū: How to Vote" |
| | "Love Letter to the Daughter I Might Have Some Day" |
| | "The Birthday Blues" |
| *Artistic Antidote* | "Ode to Stopping" |
| *Arts & Letters* | "The Birthday Effect" |
| *The Dewdrop* | "Pandemic Planner" |
| *District Lit* | "How to Be Light" |
| *Dressing Room Poetry* | "Big, Fat Pregnancy Lies" |
| *Frost Meadow Review* | "Poem for a Healthy Body" |
| *Gargoyle* | "Sonnet for the Summer" |
| *Great Lakes Review* | "Lake Superior Proposes Marriage" |
| | "Love Letter to a Friend over the Holidays" |
| *Indolent* | "Empathy Is a Preexisting Condition" |
| *The Laurel Review* | "Oh Dear God, Another Poem about Trees" |
| | "I Am a Salmon, I Am Not a Salmon" |
| *Med City Beat* | "Capitalism Q & A" |
| *Minnesota English Journal* | "Our Problems Are the Same Size as Us, and That's Okay" |
| | "I Return an Email" |
| *Quarterly West* | "How I Met Beethoven in the Psych Ward" |
| *Rattle* | "While My Husband Is in Foot Surgery During a Pandemic, I Watch Footage of the Lake Fire" |
| *Red Wheelbarrow* | "Love Poem for a California Condor" |
| *RHINO* | "The Obituary" |
| *Sunbeams* | "The Second Largest Ear of Corn in the World" |
| | "Birthday Deer, 2020: Mylar & Carrion" |
| *The Vitni Review* | "Love Letter to IUD" |

"On the 20th Anniversary of My Attempted Suicide" is anthologized in *A Tether to This World: Mental Health Recovery Stories* with Main Street Rag Publishing Company.

"Prose Aubade Ending with Lipstick" is published in the chapbook *Bright Light: Stories in the Night.*

"Another Grief Poem, Dear Reader," "Love Letter to the Daughter I Might Have Some Day," "The Birthday Blues," "The Birthday Effect," "Big, Fat Pregnancy Lies," "How I Met Beethoven in the Psych Ward," "The Obituary," "The Second Largest Ear of Corn in the World," "Love Letter to IUD," "On the 20th Anniversary of My Attempted Suicide," "Philoso-tree," "Oh Dear God, Another Poem about Trees," "Fatty, Fatty, 2 x 4," "Suicide Train," "Our Problems Are the Same Size as Us, and That's Okay," "Change is Inedible," "Anthropomorphism," and "I Am a Salmon, I Am Not a Salmon" also appear in *The Birthday Effect,* a chapbook from Black Sunflowers Poetry Press.

"How I Met Beethoven in the Psych Ward" won the AWP Intro Journals Award.

"I Am a Salmon, I Am Not a Salmon" won the League of Minnesota Poets' John Calvin Rezmerski Memorial Grand Prize.

"Philoso-tree" won the League of Minnesota Poets' Story Portage Award.

"The Obituary" was a finalist for the *RHINO* Founder's Prize.

"Love Poem for a California Condor" was a finalist for the *Red Wheelbarrow* Prize.

Many and miles of thanks to Jim Cihlar, Pam Sinicrope, all the editors of Howling Bird Press, and to Augsburg University for giving this book pages and light—I am forever honored to be part of Howling Bird Press' collection of authors.

Thank you to my husband, Brian Dean, whose support and love keeps me going each and every day, to our little "fambly." My forever gratitude goes to Christina Olson, my favorite reader, poetry advisor, and absolute inspiration—you gave me confidence in this manuscript from the start: from a pig drawn on a poem in 2004. Thanks to the beautiful Jenny Ronsman, whose writing and work and wisdom and brilliance and humor and love continually inspires. Thank you to the bright and talented Ashley Cardona, my unpaid life coach, personal designer, and classroom soulmate. I wouldn't have survived the last seventeen years without Ganglebot's Army, and all my gratitude goes to Chad Kuyper, Mike Chouinard, Liz Willingham, Bevin Shores (and the others). I love you guys. It's embarrassing how much.

I, of course, am not out of gratitude yet, and this book exists because of the Poet's Choice group: Christina Olson, Chris Haven, Dean Rader, W. Todd Kaneko, Amorak Huey, Brian Komei Dempster, Judy Halebsky, Amy McInnis, Ashley Cardona, Brian Clements, Katie Capello, and Aaron Brossiet. Your prompts led to most of this collection. Thank you to Phil Olson, who has perhaps read it about thirty times since its humble beginnings, and who taught me to teach the right way. Thank you to David Bane, Mark Ronsman, Melissa Brandt, LaToya Hozian, Ryan Clover, Lance Morgan, Shannon O'Brien, and Kristin Kingbay, and thank you to every teacher and friend who has inspired me inside the classroom and out, including the Snow Day Club: Andrea Adams, Sue Amundrud, Courtney Peterson, and Sarah Ryan. Thanks to my English department, thanks to Heather Lyke, and Nick Truxal. Thank you to my parents, Barb and Rich, and to my siblings Craig, Amanda, and Travis, for their support whenever I needed it, to Diane, whose joy makes me want to write even more, to Larry, and to Herb. Additional thanks to Minnesota State University Mankato's MFA program, particularly my poetry mentors Richard Terrill and Richard Robbins.

Thank you to the journals, presses, and judges who let these poems live on the screen and in print early on, and to the League of Minnesota Poets. Much gratitude goes to Erica Harris for her cover art and to Sierra DeMulder for her kind words.

Many thanks to my students over the years, especially the ones who shared their beautiful and inspiring creative writing with me.

And finally, thank you to Lenny, Pepper, and Beaker. Actually, thank you to every single dog that exists.

## About the Author

Jean Prokott is the author of the chapbook *The Birthday Effect*. She is a recipient of the AWP Intro Journals Award, League of Minnesota Poets Grand Prize, and two National Endowment for the Humanities scholarships. Her poetry and creative nonfiction have been published in *Arts & Letters, Rattle, RHINO,* and *Laurel Review,* among other journals. She is a graduate of Minnesota State University Mankato's MFA program, holds a Master of Science in Education from Winona State, and lives in Rochester, Minnesota.

## About Howling Bird Press

Howling Bird Press is the publishing house of Augsburg University's Master of Fine Arts in Creative Writing program. We offer an annual book contest in alternating genres: poetry, fiction, and nonfiction. The contest is open to emerging and established authors, and receives submissions from across the country. The author is awarded a cash prize, book publication, and an invitation to read at the MFA program's summer residency in Minneapolis. Our previous books are *Self, Divided* by John Medeiros, winner of the 2020 Nonfiction Prize; *Irreversible Things* by Lisa Van Orman Hadley, winner of the 2019 Fiction Prize; *Simples* by KateLynn Hibbard, winner of the 2018 Poetry Prize; *Still Life with Horses* by Jean Harper, winner of the 2017 Nonfiction Prize; *The Topless Widow of Herkimer Street* by Jacob M. Appel, winner of the 2016 Fiction Prize; and *At the Border of Wilshire & Nobody* by Marci Vogel, winner of the 2015 Poetry Prize. Howling Bird Press books are distributed by Small Press Distribution; they are available online and in fine bookstores everywhere.

Howling Bird Press acknowledges our editors Motunrayo Fakuwajo, Katrina Gabelko, Arabella Hearley, Aaliyah Herrion, Katelyn Holman, Megan Kosse, Nicholas Lindstrom, Lucas Miller, and Pam Sinicrope. The press also thanks MFA Director Stephan Clark, Associate Director Lindsay Starck, Poetry Mentor Heid E. Erdrich, and all the faculty, mentors, staff, and students of Augsburg's MFA in Creative Writing. We thank English Department Chair Mzenga Wanyama, the English Department faculty, Dean of Arts and Sciences Ryan Haaland, Dean of Professional Studies and Graduate Programs Monica Devers, Provost and Senior Vice President for Academic and Student Affairs Karen Kaivola, and Augsburg University President Paul Pribbenow. Special thanks to the contributors to the Howling Bird Press Publishing Fund, who—through Augsburg's Give to the Max campaign—provided generous support for this year's project, including Laurie R. Anderson, Jacob M. Appel, Betty A. Christiansen, James Cihlar, Norman J. Crampton, Cass Dalglish, David de Young, History Through Fiction, Katherine M. Fagen, James P. Lenfestey, Diana Lopez Jones, Paul C. Pribbenow, Thomas Redshaw, Jennifer A. Shutt, and Lisa Van Orman Hadley.